# ABC Print Handwriting Practice Book for kids

## Preschool writing Workbook for Pre K
## Kindergarten and Kids Ages 3-5

© Copyright TCEC Publishing 2021 – All rights reserved.

The content contained within this book may not be reproduced, duplicated or transmitted without direct written permission from the author or the publisher.

Under no circumstance will any blame or legal responsibility be held against the publisher, or author, for any damages, reparation, or monetary loss due to the information contained within this book. Either directly or indirectly.

Legal Notice:

This book is copyright protected. This book is only for personal use. You cannot amend, distribute, sell, use, quote or paraphrase any part, or the content within this book, without the consent of the author or publisher.

Disclaimer

Please note the information contained within this document is for educational and entertainment purpose only. All effort has been executed to present accurate, up to date, and reliable, complete information. No warranties of any kind are declared or implied.

**appel**

Aa Aa Aa Aa

Aa Aa Aa Aa

Aa Aa Aa Aa

Aa Aa Aa Aa

**appel**

Aa Aa Aa Aa

Aa Aa Aa Aa

Aa Aa Aa Aa

Aa Aa Aa Aa

Try writing these words one at a time.

*Apple* *Apple* *Apple*

*Apple* *Apple* *Apple*

*apple* *apple* *apple*

*apple* *apple* *apple*

Try writing these words one at a time.

*Apple Apple Apple*

*Apple Apple Apple*

*apple apple apple*

*apple apple apple*

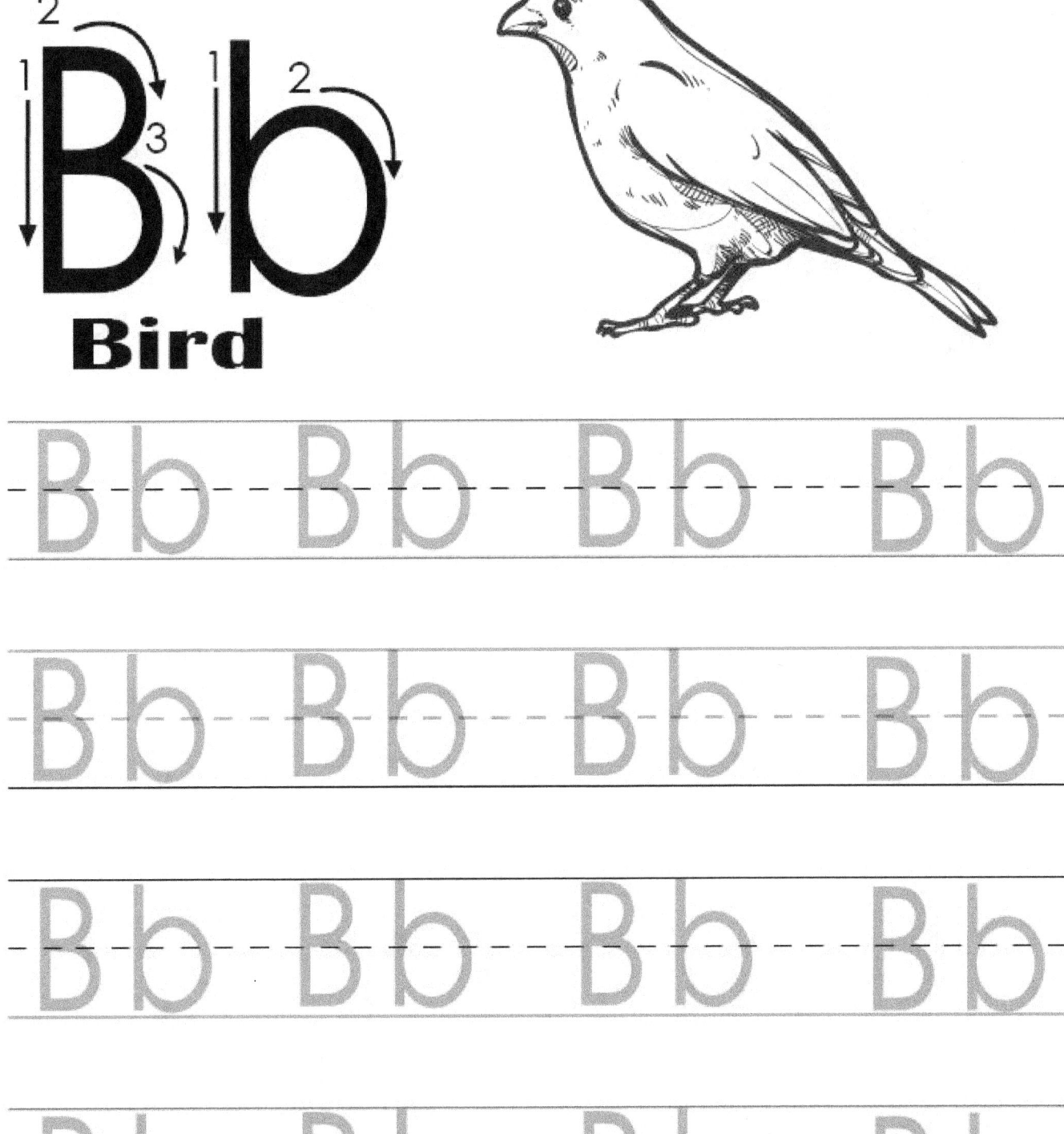

Try writing these words one at a time.

*Bear Bear Bear Bear*

*Bear Bear Bear*

*bear bear bear bear*

*bear bear bear*

Try writing these words one at a time.

*Bear Bear Bear Bear*

*Bear Bear Bear*

*bear bear bear bear*

*bear bear bear*

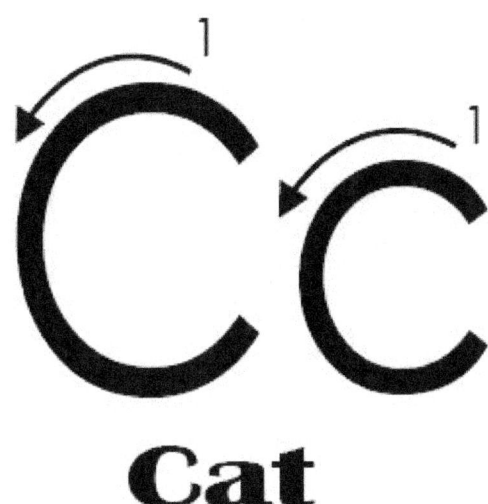

**Cat**

Cc Cc Cc Cc Cc

Cc Cc Cc Cc Cc

Cc Cc Cc Cc Cc

Cc Cc Cc Cc Cc

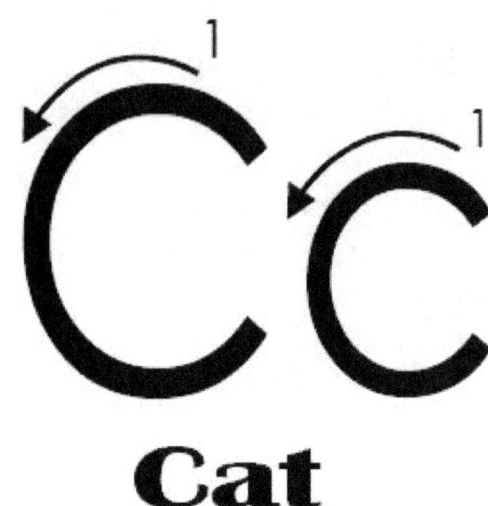
**Cat**

Try writing these words one at a time.

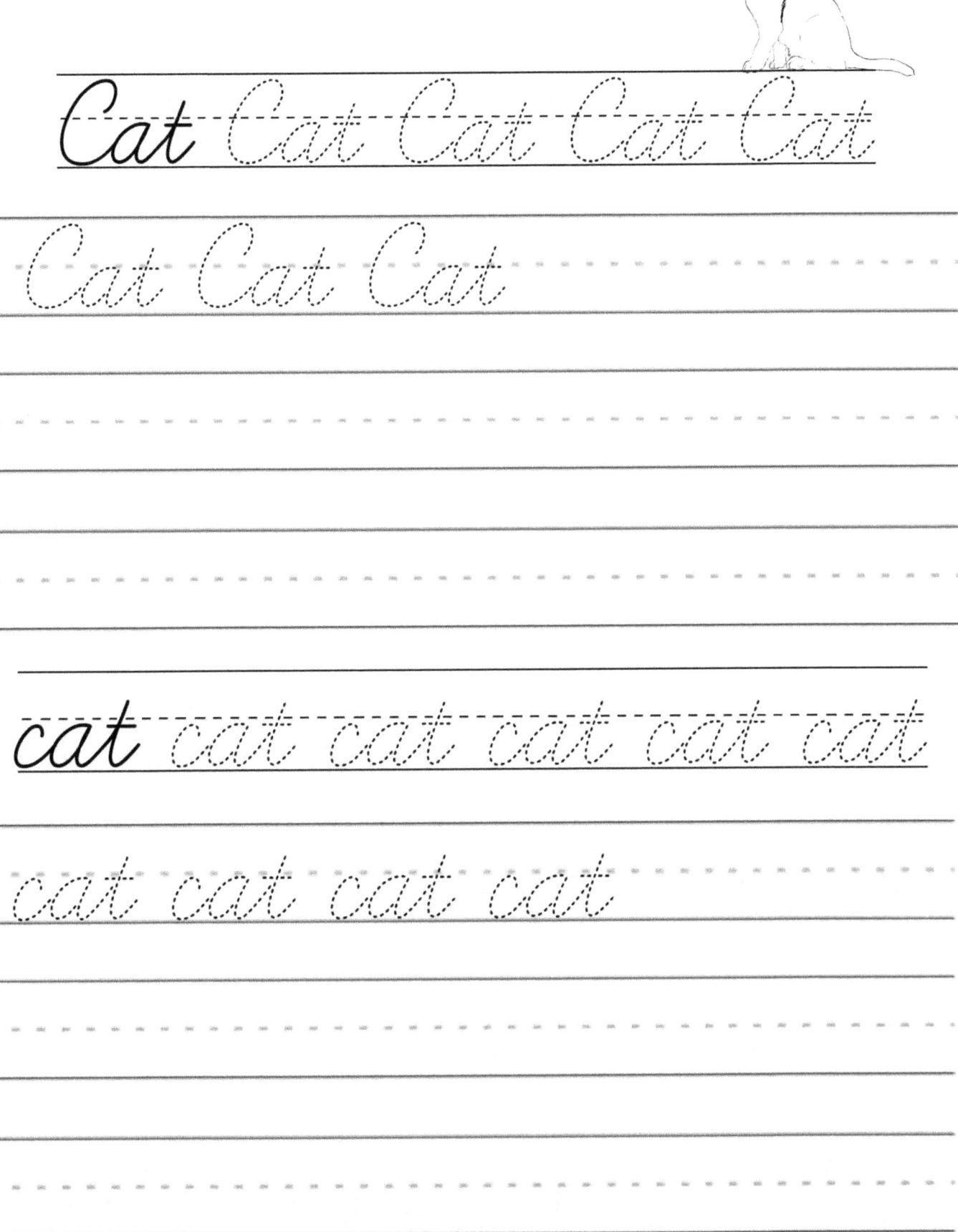

Try writing these words one at a time.

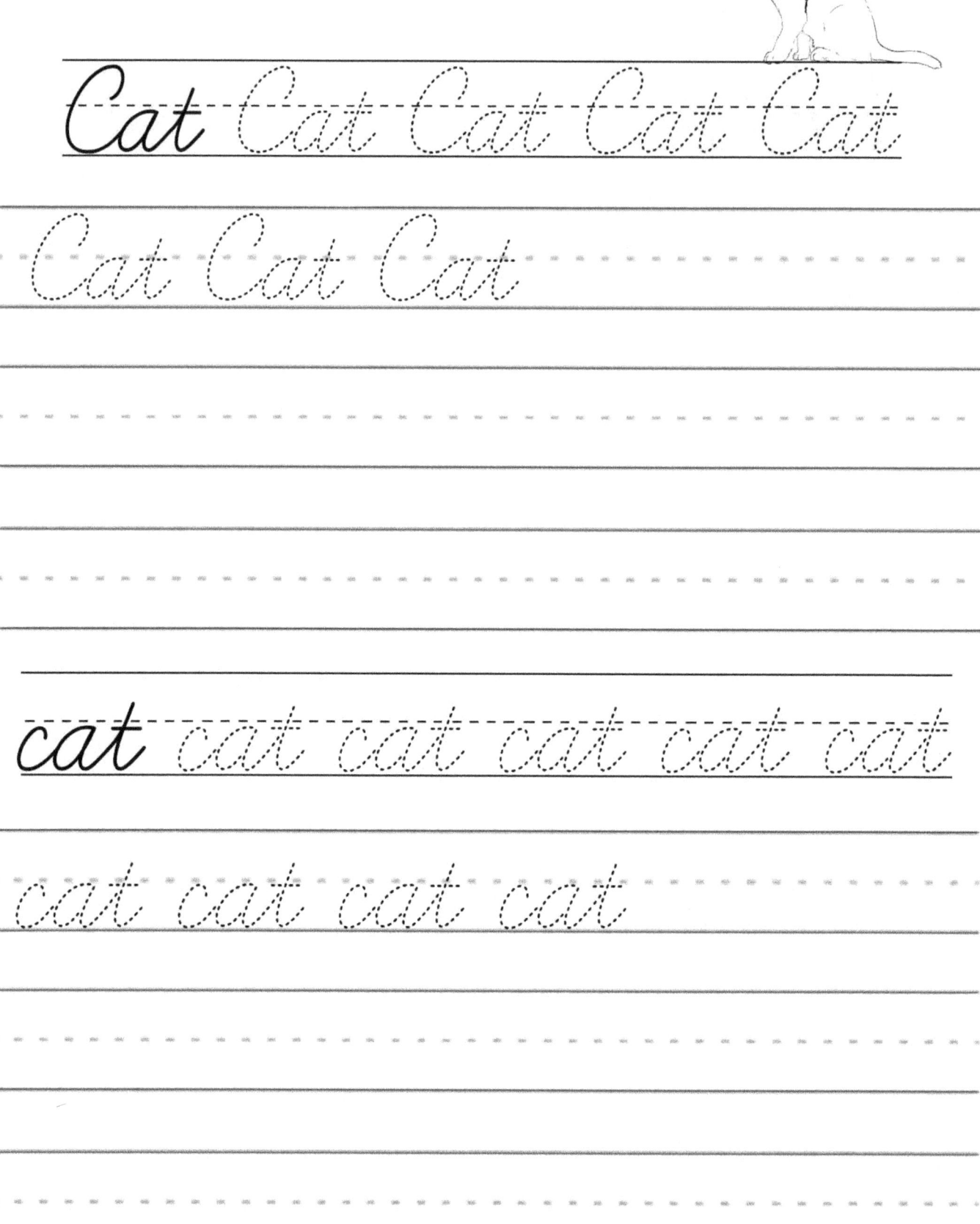

**Dog**

Dd Dd Dd Dd

Dd Dd Dd Dd

Dd Dd Dd Dd

Dd Dd Dd Dd

**Dog**

Try writing these words one at a time.

Dog Dog Dog Dog Dog

Dog Dog Dog

dog dog dog dog dog

dog dog dog

Try writing these words one at a time.

*Dog Dog Dog Dog Dog*

*Dog Dog Dog*

*dog dog dog dog dog*

*dog dog dog*

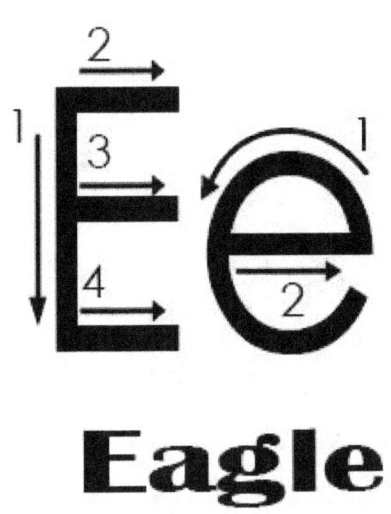

**Eagle**

Ee Ee Ee Ee

Ee Ee Ee Ee

Ee Ee Ee Ee

Ee Ee Ee Ee

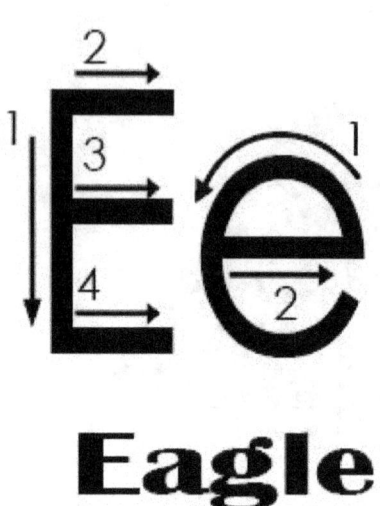

**Eagle**

Ee Ee Ee Ee Ee

Ee Ee Ee Ee Ee

Ee Ee Ee Ee Ee

Ee Ee Ee Ee Ee

Try writing these words one at a time.

*Egg* *Egg* *Egg* *Egg* *Egg*
*Egg* *Egg* *Egg*

*egg* *egg* *egg* *egg* *egg*
*egg* *egg* *egg*

**Try writing these words one at a time.**

*Egg Egg Egg Egg Egg*

*Egg Egg Egg*

*egg egg egg egg egg*

*egg egg egg*

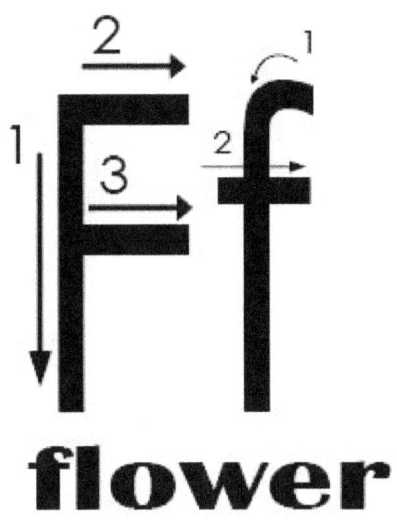
**flower**

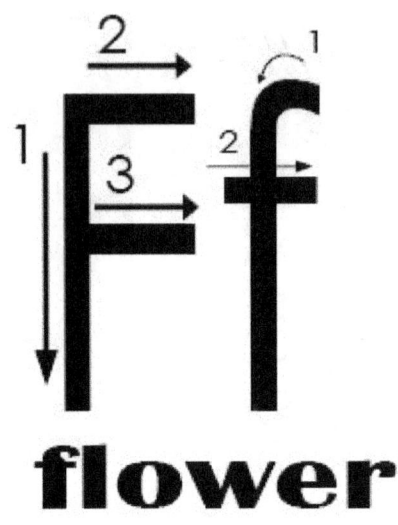

**flower**

Ff Ff Ff Ff

Ff Ff Ff Ff

Ff Ff Ff Ff

Ff Ff Ff Ff

Try writing these words one at a time.

*Fish Fish Fish Fish*

*Fish Fish Fish*

*fish fish fish fish fish*

*fish fish fish*

Try writing these words one at a time.

*Fish Fish Fish Fish*

*Fish Fish Fish*

*fish fish fish fish fish*

*fish fish fish*

**giraffe**

Gg Gg Gg Gg

Gg Gg Gg Gg

Gg Gg Gg Gg

Gg Gg Gg Gg

**giraffe**

Gg Gg Gg Gg Gg

Gg Gg Gg Gg Gg

Gg Gg Gg Gg Gg

Gg Gg Gg Gg Gg

Try writing these words one at a time.

*Quail Quail Quail*

*Quail Quail Quail*

*quail quail quail quail*

*quail quail quail*

**Try writing these words one at a time.**

*Quail Quail Quail*

*Quail Quail Quail*

*quail quail quail quail*

*quail quail quail*

Try writing these words one at a time.

*House House House*

*House House House*

*house house house*

*house house house*

Try writing these words one at a time.

*House House House*

*House House House*

*house house house*

*house house house*

Try writing these words one at a time.

*Goat Goat Goat Goat*

*Goat Goat Goat*

*goat goat goat goat*

*goat goat goat*

Try writing these words one at a time.

*Goat Goat Goat Goat*

*Goat Goat Goat*

*goat goat goat goat*

*goat goat goat*

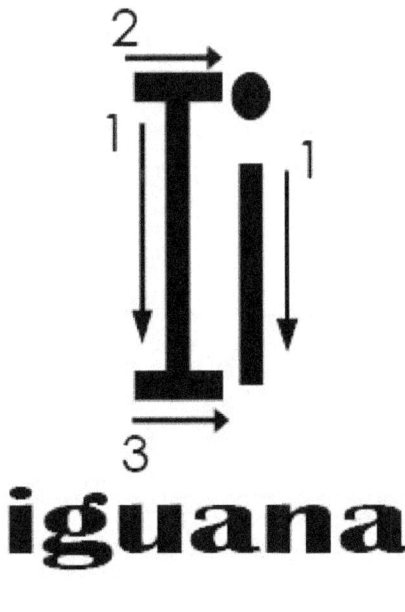
**iguana**

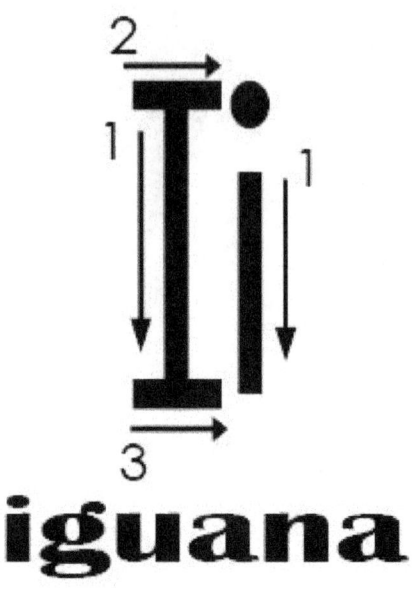

**iguana**

Try writing these words one at a time.

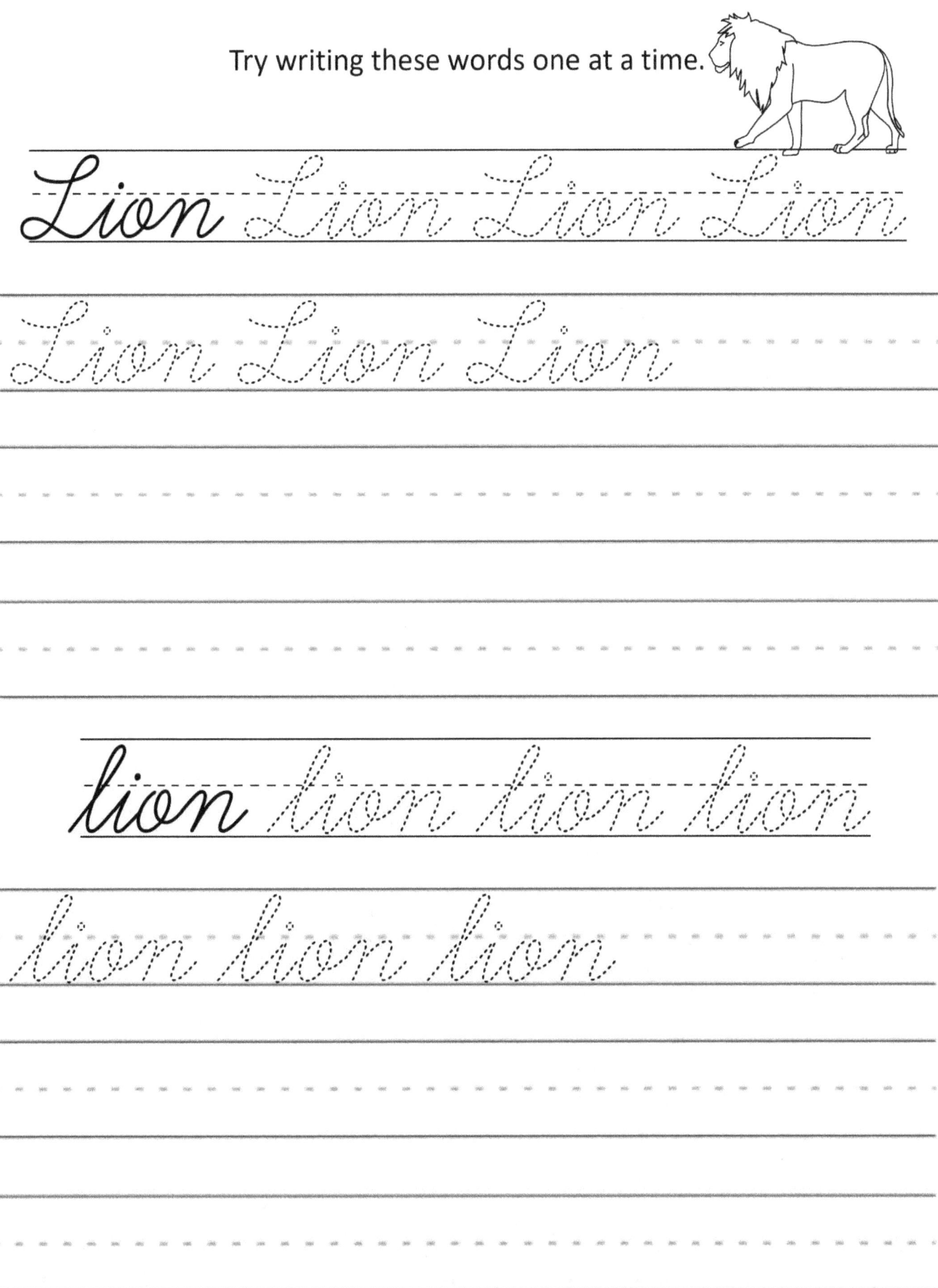

Try writing these words one at a time.

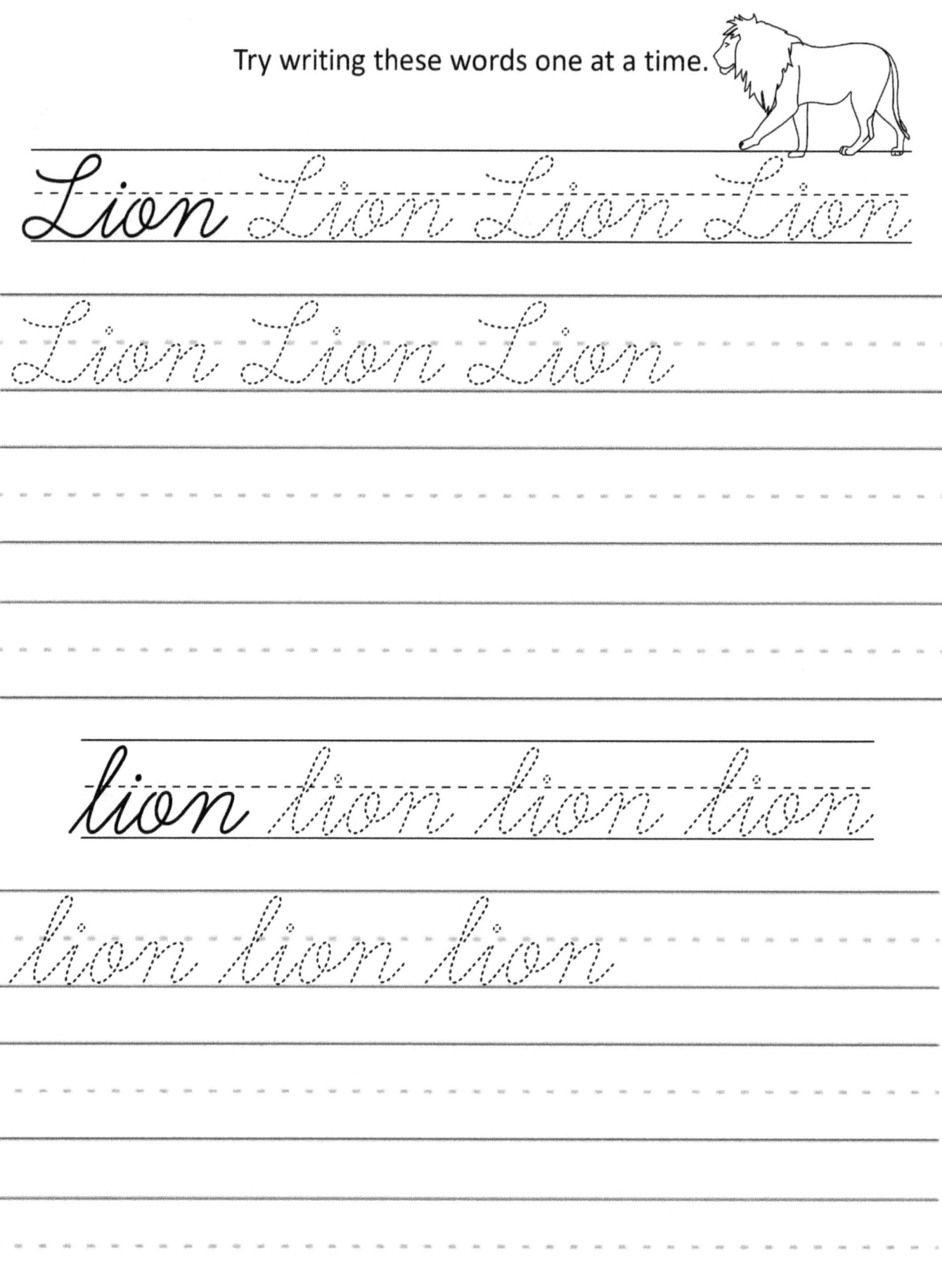

# Jj
**jellyfish**

Jj Jj Jj Jj Jj

Jj Jj Jj Jj Jj

Jj Jj Jj Jj Jj

Jj Jj Jj Jj Jj

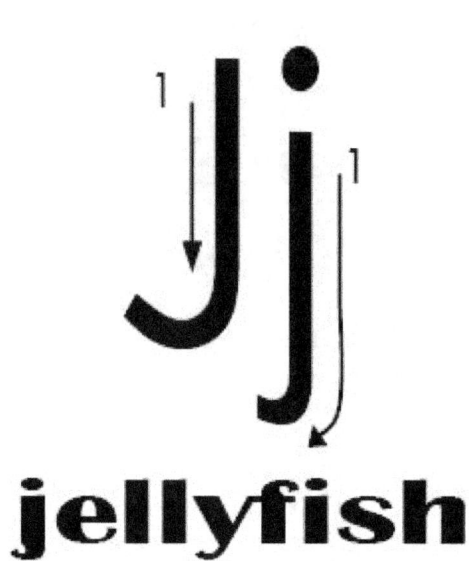

**jellyfish**

Jj Jj Jj Jj Jj

Jj Jj Jj Jj Jj

Jj Jj Jj Jj Jj

Jj Jj Jj Jj Jj

Try writing these words one at a time.

*Juice* *Juice* *Juice* *Juice*

*Juice* *Juice* *Juice*

*juice* *juice* *juice* *juice*

*juice* *juice* *juice*

Try writing these words one at a time.

**kangaroo**

Kk Kk Kk Kk

Kk Kk Kk Kk

Kk Kk Kk Kk

Kk Kk Kk Kk

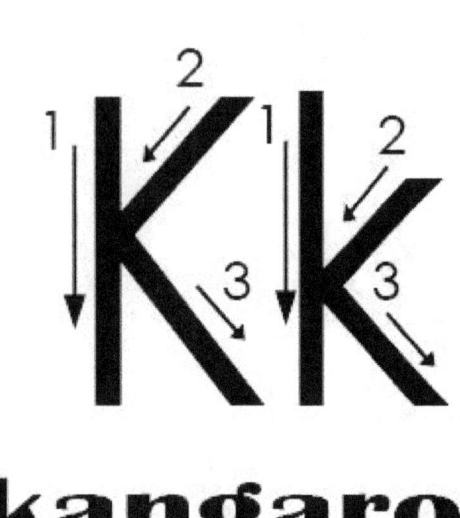

**kangaroo**

Kk Kk Kk Kk

Kk Kk Kk Kk

Kk Kk Kk Kk

Kk Kk Kk Kk

Try writing these words one at a time.

Kite Kite Kite Kite Kite

Kite Kite Kite

kite kite kite kite kite

kite kite kite

Try writing these words one at a time.

*Kite* Kite Kite Kite Kite

Kite Kite Kite

*kite* kite kite kite kite

kite kite kite

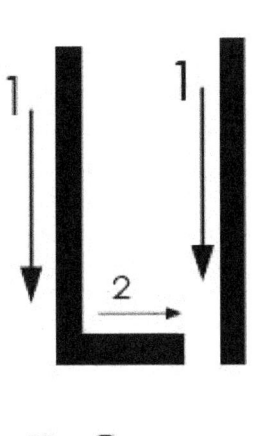

**Lion**

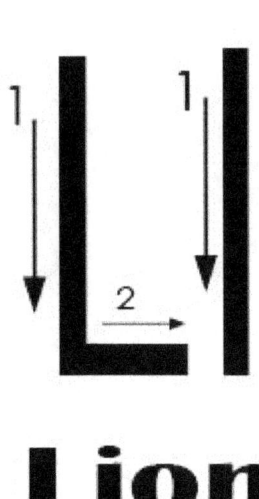

**Lion**

Try writing these words one at a time.

*igloo  igloo  igloo  igloo*

*igloo  igloo  igloo*

*igloo  igloo  igloo  igloo*

*igloo  igloo  igloo*

Try writing these words one at a time.

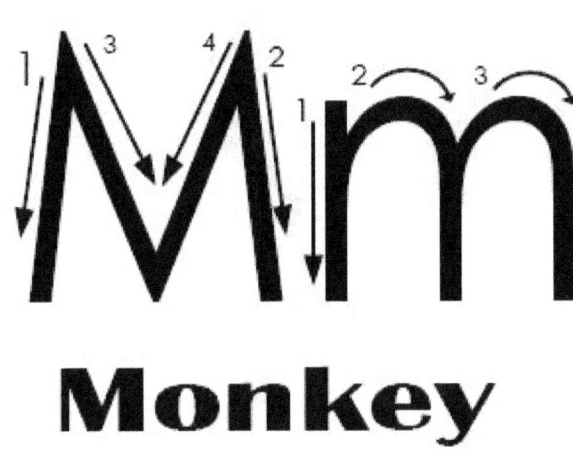

**Monkey**

Mm  Mm  Mm

Mm  Mm  Mm

Mm  Mm  Mm

Mm  Mm  Mm

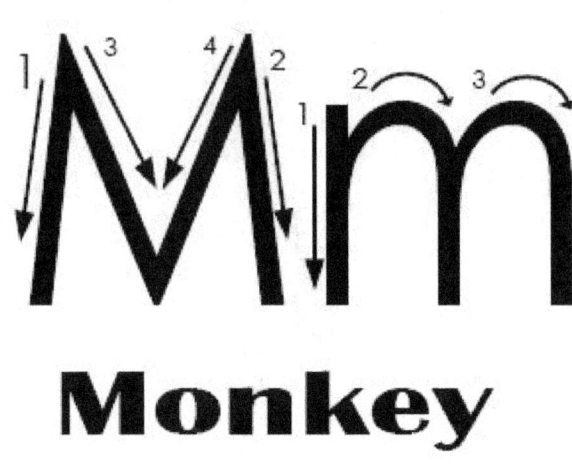

**Monkey**

Mm Mm Mm

Mm Mm Mm

Mm Mm Mm

Mm Mm Mm

Try writing these words one at a time.

*Mouse Mouse Mouse*

*Mouse Mouse Mouse*

*mouse mouse mouse*

*mouse mouse mouse*

Try writing these words one at a time.

*Mouse Mouse Mouse*

*Mouse Mouse Mouse*

*mouse mouse mouse*

*mouse mouse mouse*

**narwhal**

Nn Nn Nn Nn

Nn Nn Nn Nn

Nn Nn Nn Nn

Nn Nn Nn Nn

narwhal

Nn Nn Nn Nn

Nn Nn Nn Nn

Nn Nn Nn Nn

Nn Nn Nn Nn

Try writing these words one at a time.

Nest Nest Nest Nest

Nest Nest Nest

nest nest nest nest

nest nest nest

Try writing these words one at a time.

*Nest Nest Nest Nest*

*Nest Nest Nest*

*nest nest nest nest*

*nest nest nest*

**OWL**

**OWL**

Try writing these words one at a time.

*Owl Owl Owl Owl*

*Owl Owl Owl*

*owl owl owl owl owl*

*owl owl owl*

Try writing these words one at a time.

*Owl Owl Owl Owl*

*Owl Owl Owl*

*owl owl owl owl owl*

*owl owl owl*

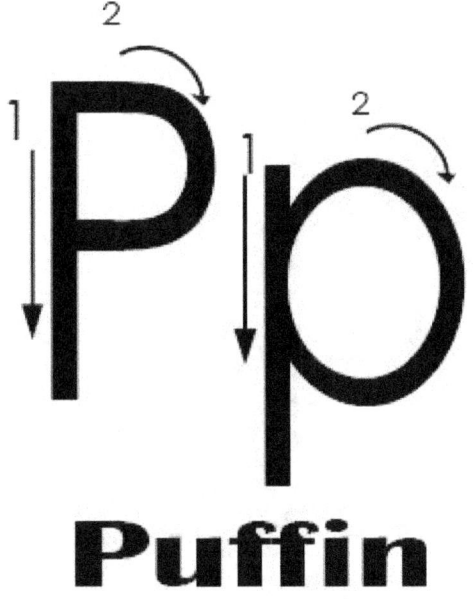

**Puffin**

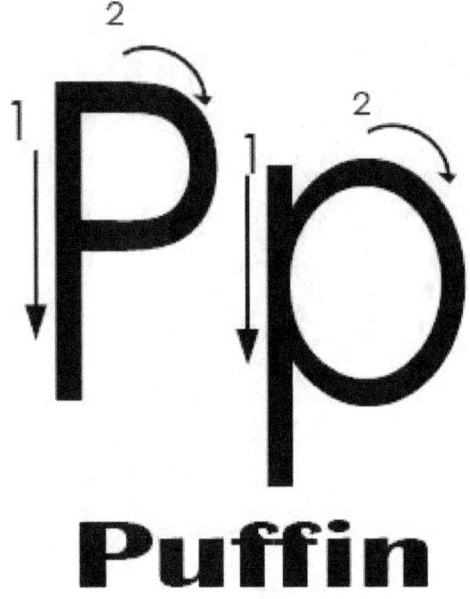

**Puffin**

Pp Pp Pp Pp Pp

Pp Pp Pp Pp Pp

Pp Pp Pp Pp Pp

Pp Pp Pp Pp Pp

Try writing these words one at a time.

*Plane Plane Plane*

*Plane Plane Plane*

*plane plane plane*

*plane plane plane*

Try writing these words one at a time.

*Plane Plane Plane*

*Plane Plane Plane*

*plane plane plane*

*plane plane plane*

**Quail**

**Quail**

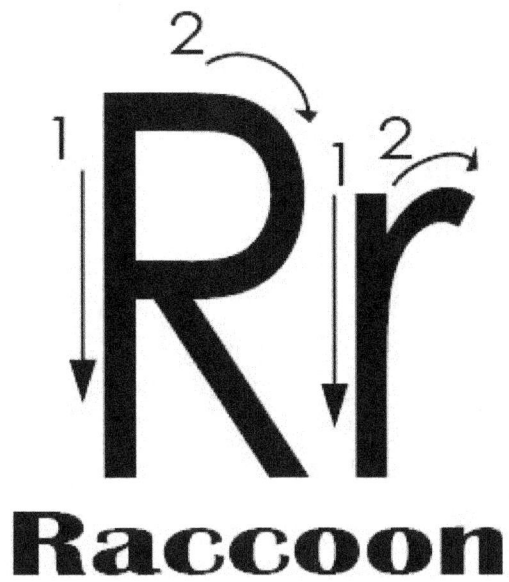

**Raccoon**

Rr Rr Rr Rr Rr

Rr Rr Rr Rr Rr

Rr Rr Rr Rr Rr

Rr Rr Rr Rr Rr

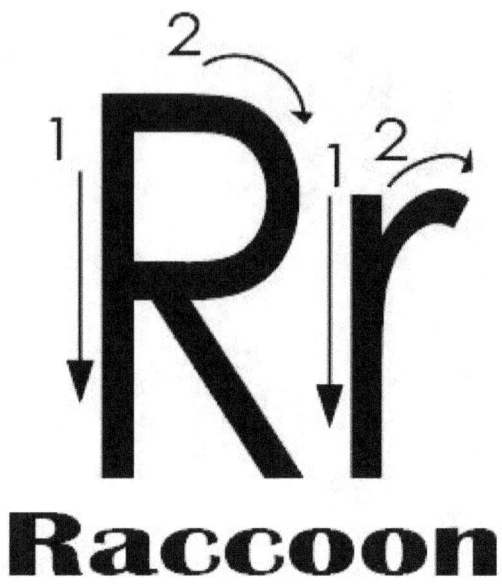

**Raccoon**

Rr Rr Rr Rr Rr

Rr Rr Rr Rr Rr

Rr Rr Rr Rr Rr

Rr Rr Rr Rr Rr

Try writing these words one at a time.

*Rose Rose Rose Rose*

*Rose Rose Rose*

*rose rose rose rose rose*

*rose rose rose*

Try writing these words one at a time.

*Rose Rose Rose Rose*

*Rose Rose Rose*

*rose rose rose rose rose*

*rose rose rose*

**Snake**

Ss　Ss　Ss　Ss

Ss　Ss　Ss　Ss

Ss　Ss　Ss　Ss

Ss　Ss　Ss　Ss

**Snake**

Ss Ss Ss Ss

Ss Ss Ss Ss

Ss Ss Ss Ss

Ss Ss Ss Ss

Try writing these words one at a time.

*Sun* Sun Sun Sun

Sun Sun Sun

*sun* sun sun sun sun

sun sun sun

Try writing these words one at a time.

*Sun Sun Sun Sun*

*Sun Sun Sun*

*sun sun sun sun sun*

*sun sun sun*

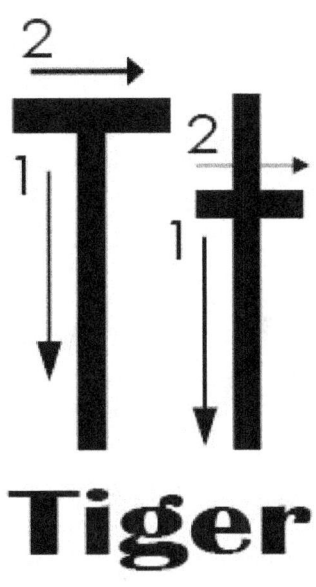

**Tiger**

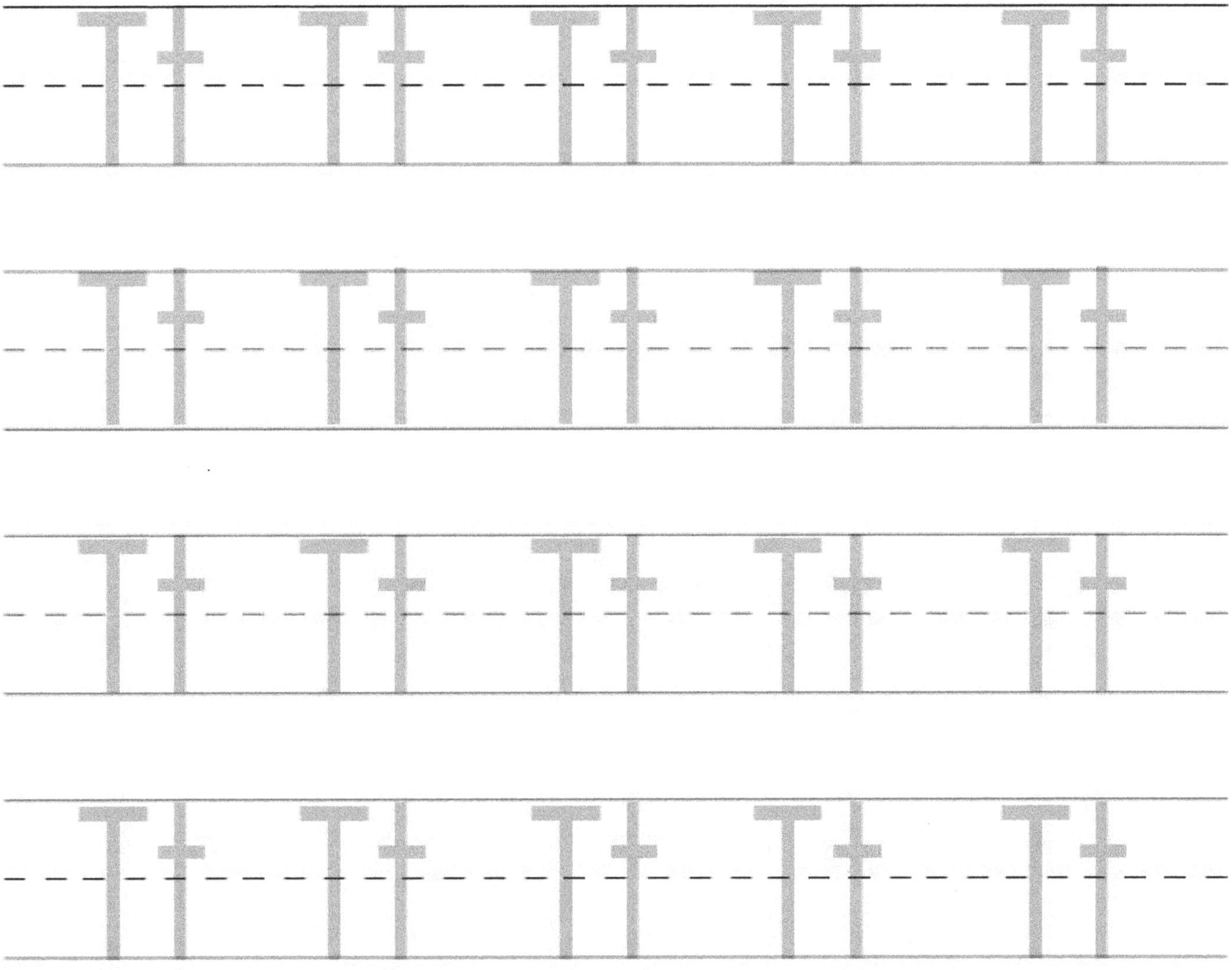

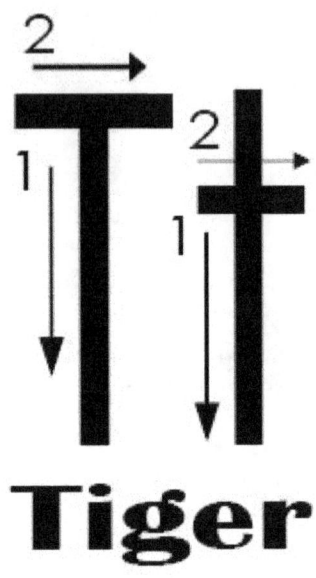

**Tiger**

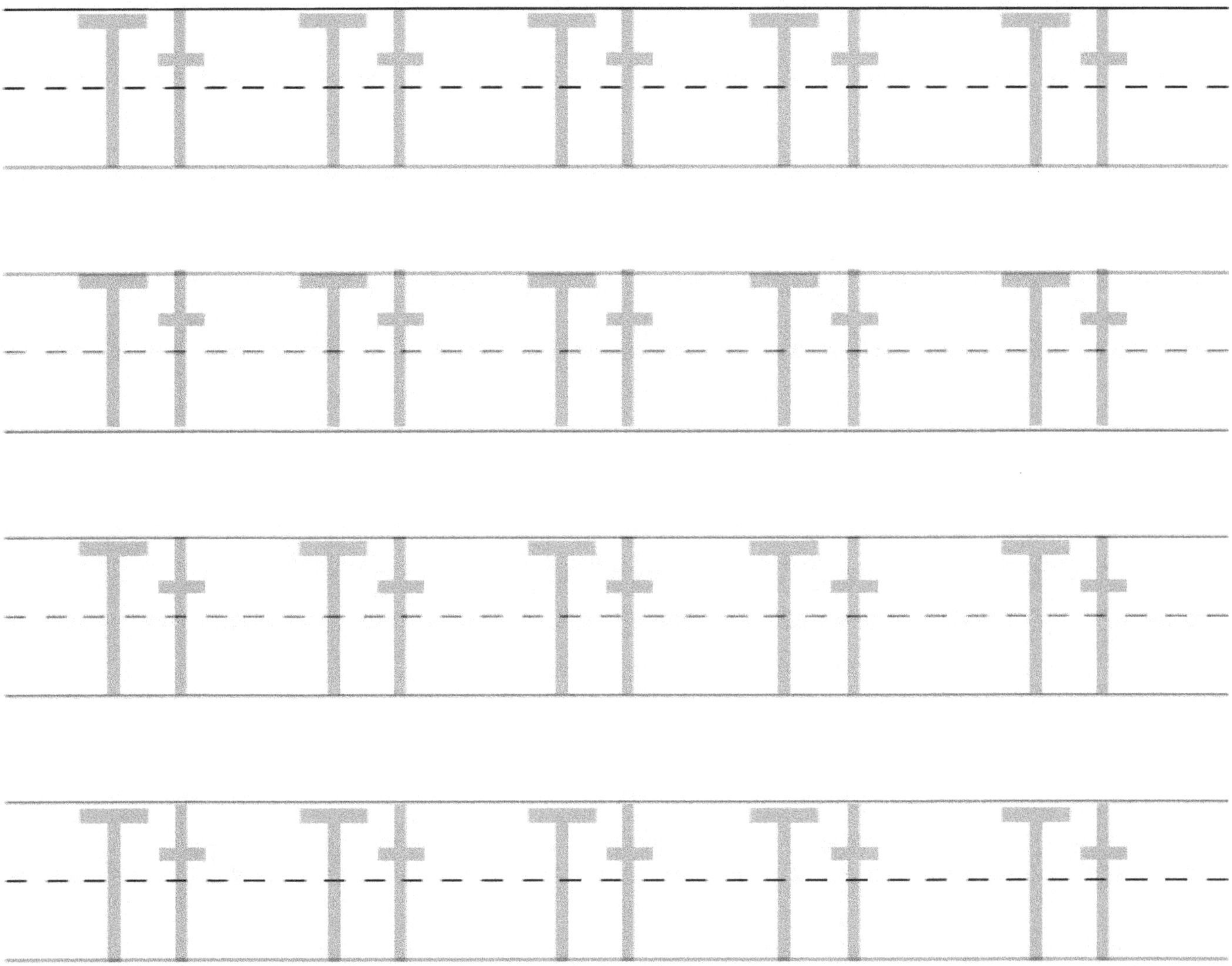

Try writing these words one at a time.

*Tent Tent Tent Tent*

*Tent Tent Tent*

*tent tent tent tent*

*tent tent tent*

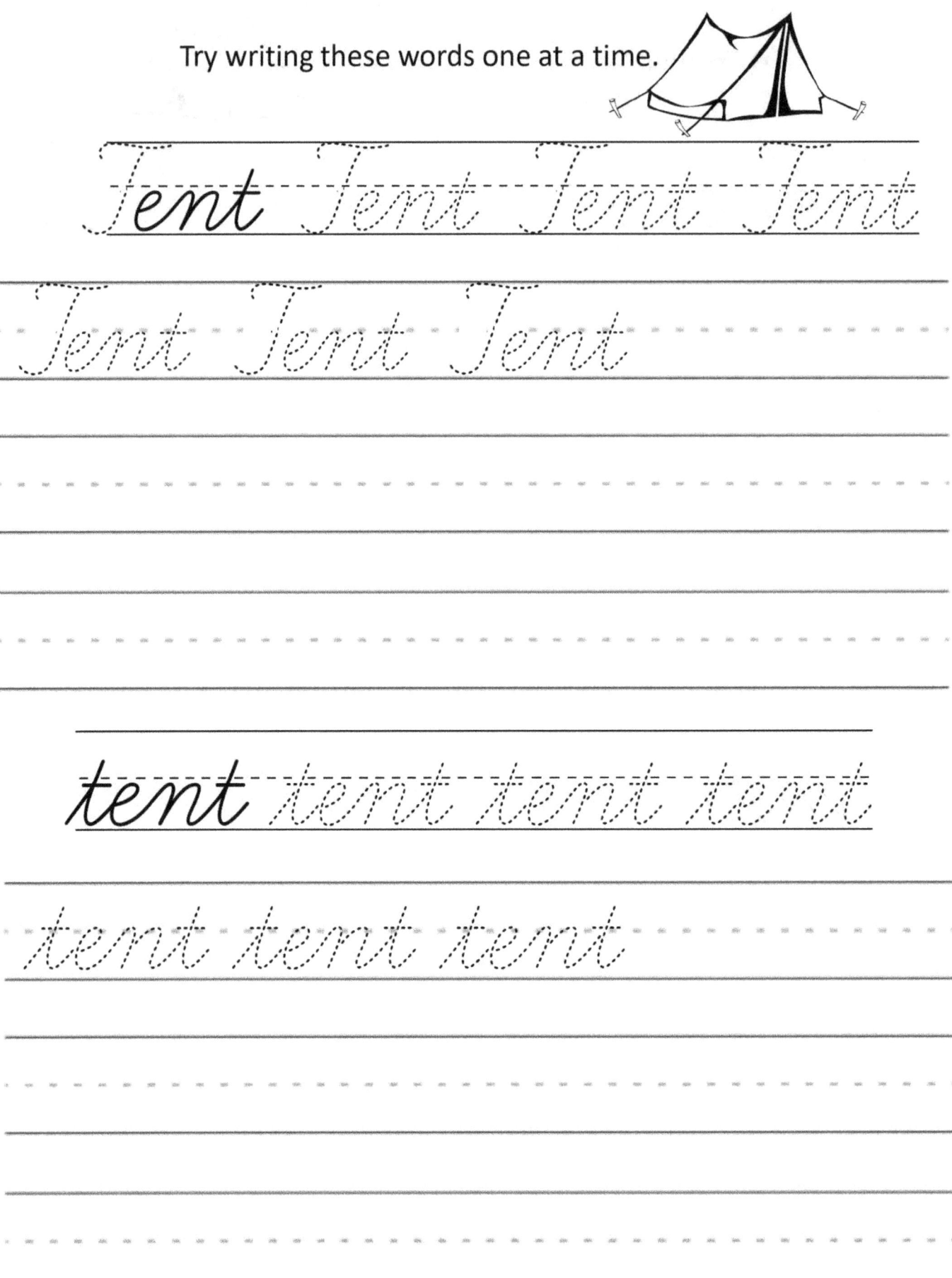

Try writing these words one at a time.

# Uu
**Unicorn**

Uu Uu Uu Uu

Uu Uu Uu Uu

Uu Uu Uu Uu

Uu Uu Uu Uu

# Uu
## Unicorn

Try writing these words one at a time.

*Up Up Up Up Up Up*

*Up Up Up*

*up up up up up up up*

*up up up*

Try writing these words one at a time.

*Up Up Up Up Up Up*

*Up Up Up*

*up up up up up up up*

*up up up*

**vampire bat**

**vampire bat**

Try writing these words one at a time.

*Van Van Van Van*

*Van Van Van*

*van van van van*

*van van van*

**Try writing these words one at a time.**

*Van Van Van Van*

*Van Van Van*

*van van van van*

*van van van*

**Ww** 
**Worm**

Ww Ww Ww

Ww Ww Ww

Ww Ww Ww

Ww Ww Ww

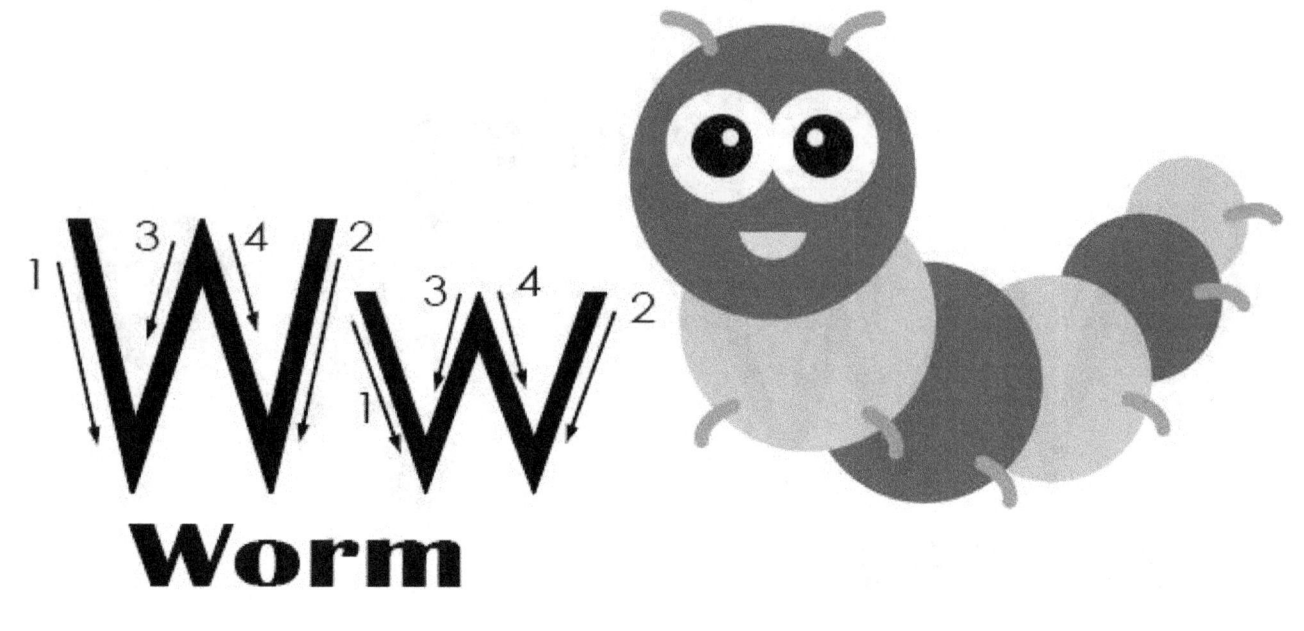

**Worm**

Try writing these words one at a time.

**Try writing these words one at a time.**

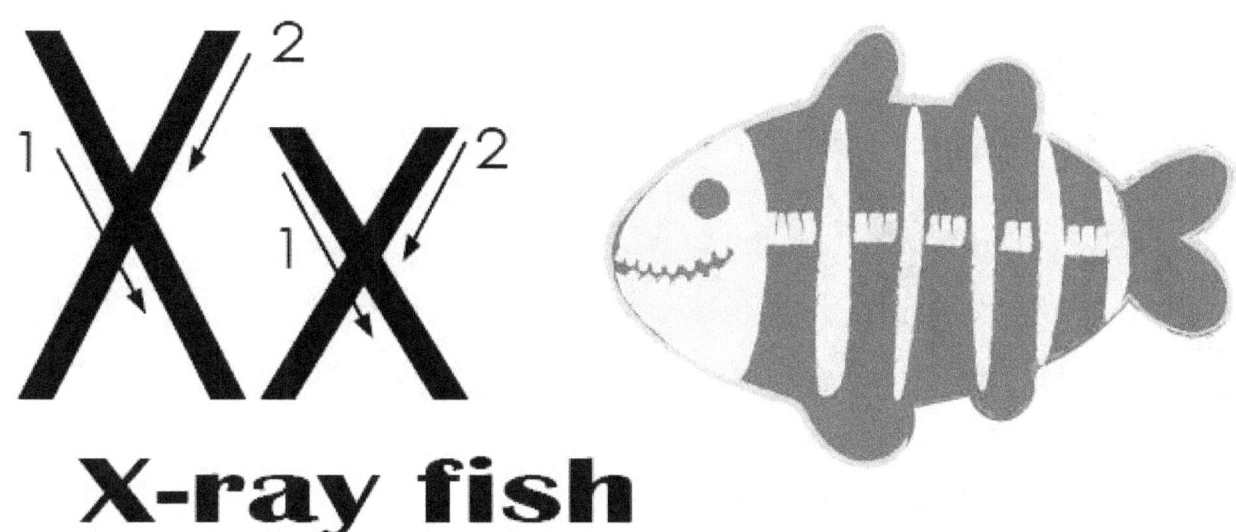

**X-ray fish**

**X-ray fish**

Try writing these words one at a time.

CAT XING

*Xing Xing Xing Xing*

*Xing Xing*

*xing xing xing xing*

*xing xing xing*

Try writing these words one at a time.

*Xing Xing Xing Xing*

*Xing Xing*

*xing xing xing xing*

*xing xing xing*

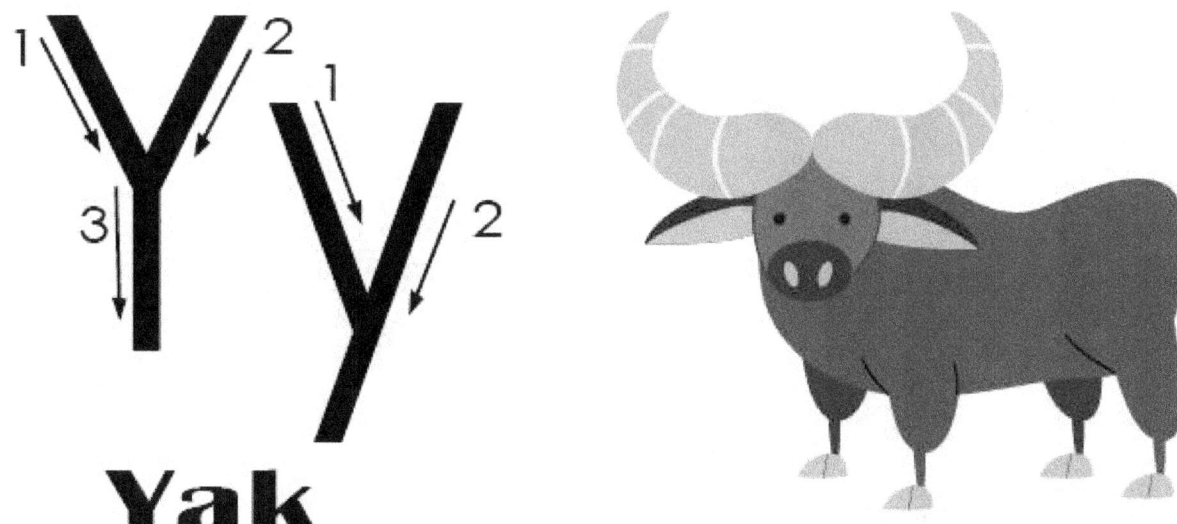

**Yak**

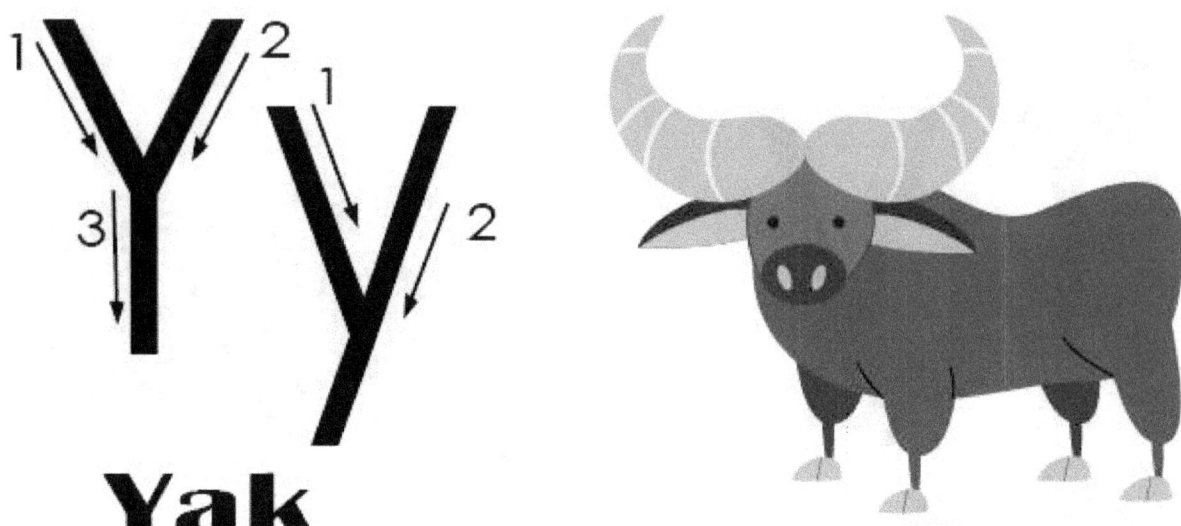

**Yak**

Yy Yy Yy Yy Yy

Yy Yy Yy Yy Yy

Yy Yy Yy Yy Yy

Yy Yy Yy Yy Yy

Try writing these words one at a time.

*Yam Yam Yam Yam*

*Yam Yam Yam*

*yam yam yam yam*

*yam yam yam*

**Try writing these words one at a time.**

*Yam Yam Yam Yam*

*Yam Yam Yam*

*yam yam yam yam*

*yam yam yam*

# Zz
**Zebra**

# Zz
### Zebra

Try writing these words one at a time.

*Zebra Zebra Zebra*

*Zebra Zebra Zebra*

*zebra zebra zebra*

*zebra zebra zebra*

**Try writing these words one at a time.**

*Zebra Zebra Zebra*

*Zebra Zebra Zebra*

*zebra zebra zebra*

*zebra zebra zebra*

1 1 1 1 1 1 1 1 1 1

2 2 2 2 2 2

3 3 3 3 3 3 3

4 4 4 4 4 4 4

3 3 3 3 3 3 3

4 4 4 4 4 4 4

5 5 5 5 5 5 5

6 6 6 6 6 6 6

5 5 5 5 5 5 5

6 6 6 6 6 6 6

7 7 7 7 7 7 7

8 8 8 8 8 8 8

7 7 7 7 7 7 7

8 8 8 8 8 8 8 8

9 9 9 9 9 9 9

0 0 0 0 0 0 0

9 9 9 9 9 9 9

0 0 0 0 0 0 0

www.ingramcontent.com/pod-product-compliance
Lightning Source LLC
Chambersburg PA
CBHW081347080526
44588CB00016B/2407